We Make A Difference:

Discovering The Power Of Our Though

Introduction:

I am excited to be writing this book.

This is about how powerful we are even if we don't think we are.

What we say and do, does make a difference.

This book is part of an experiment.

I am asking people to become more aware of their thoughts.

When we do this, we discover something amazing.

We are valuable and we can make a difference.

This book explores how powerful our thoughts are.

A thought I had regarding spreading the word about this book was to ask people to:

'Buy One, Tell Two, And Review!'

That would be a great way to pass on these ideas so more and more people realise how powerful they are.

Please consider buying a copy of this book. Tell two other people about the book and ask them to do the same. Please visit Amazon and review the book.

Positive reviews really help more people discover a book exists.

I will donate 50 per cent of the profits from every copy sold to a worthy cause.

I have an organisation in mind that is close to my heart, and I know they will make good use of any funds that they receive.

I will tell you all about it very soon!

I have some exciting ideas that I am looking forward to sharing with you too.

Before I do that, let me tell you how this all works:

Chapter One: The Thought Effect

That would make a good title for a book in its own right, but I like it as a chapter heading too.

The thoughts that we have can have a significant impact on our lives.

In a way, we create our world from within.

What do I mean by this?

If we have a thought, we can choose to act on it or let it go.

We label some thoughts as positive as they make us feel good.

Other thoughts can make us feel stressed or upset. We tend to label them as negative.

We can get stuck in negative thought cycles sometimes, and this can really bring us down.

We often take our thoughts seriously and spend a lot of time focused on them. We sometimes forget that we are not our thoughts. We have thoughts. Once we realise this, we can choose which thoughts to focus on, and which ones to accept and then release.

Our thoughts have a powerful impact on us and on the people around us.

Sometimes someone has a thought, and they choose to act on it. They have an idea for an exciting invention, for example.

These thoughts, when acted upon, really can change the world.

Look around you at all your possessions. Someone created each one of them.

Humans are fantastically creative and have the potential to do wonderful things.

We often notice the things that are challenging or unpleasant in the world, but good things are happening all around us too. Sometimes all this goodness goes unnoticed, but it is there none the less.

Chapter 2: Possible, Impossible

At one point I was going to call this book 'Possible Impossible Dream' but then I realised that someone had written a book with a similar title. I found this a little frustrating at first, but then I found it oddly comforting.

Someone else has realised that the seemingly impossible can become possible. They had the thoughts necessary to create the title and to write the book.

Once I realised there was a book with this title, I decided to read it. It was very interesting.

I started to wonder if other people had similar thoughts for similar books.

It is good to know that there are people out there who believe that it is possible for us to change things for the better.

A lot of the time we have thoughts and ideas. If we consider that they aren't possible we are likely to reject them.

Sometimes someone thinks something is impossible only to find that someone else considers that the thing is possible and so they create or invent it.

We can miss out on a lot of opportunities and experiences if we dismiss an idea as impossible without fully considering whether this is true.

Items such as computers and phones were ideas that people acted on.

Perhaps other people had similar ideas but decided not to act on them.

If you think of something that you would like to do, why not try it out?

It may or may not work out, but you will never know unless you try.

Chapter 3: Inner Revolution

When I started thinking about this book, I did consider calling it 'Inner Revolution.'

It turned out someone had claimed that title too.

This was initially annoying, but then I considered that maybe it is rather exciting.

Does this mean that other people are thinking along the same lines as me?

Do you believe that if we want change, we need to change our focus?

That is what I am starting to realise.

I am delighted with the realisation that other people have had similar thoughts to me and acted upon them. They have turned a thought into a form of reality by creating books.

During my personal development journey, I have heard people say that thoughts become things. I think Bob Proctor originally said it.

If you haven't heard of Bob Proctor, Google him. Bob Proctor was an inspiring man. You might enjoy finding out more about him.

Thinking of an idea for a book, writing and publishing the book is a great example of 'thoughts becoming things.'

I also love the idea that anyone can pick up your book and read your thoughts. If they like your ideas, they can adopt and develop them. They can follow your example and spread the word. If they don't feel inspired or even interested in your ideas, they can put the book down and move on.

I have discovered that all thoughts really are things. That includes thoughts that we label as negative.

Negative Thoughts:

When we think of a 'negative' thought we can feel bad. We don't like feeling bad and we don't always realise that these difficult feelings are a useful tool. They offer a clue about the thought we are having. If we don't like feeling a certain way, we can let certain thoughts go and choose to focus on new ones. That sounds simple and yet it isn't.

We don't need to deny or suppress our uncomfortable feelings. They are helping to alert us to thoughts that can affect our behaviours. They can help us to decide if we need to take any action or whether we can decide to let some things go.

An example of this might be that a friend says something unkind to us and we feel bad. We think that everyone agrees with our friend, and this makes us feel terrible.

It is important to recognise how we feel. This can help us decide to take action. We might decide to let the friend know how we are feeling. Our friend might apologise. Perhaps they didn't realise how upset we felt after hearing their comment.

We have all sorts of thoughts entering and leaving our heads. What we don't always realise is we can choose to focus on the good ones.

Have you got some ideas and dreams that you would like to act upon?

According to research, the average person will have around 60,000 thoughts a day. Some are important, while others can be ridiculous. We don't have to take them all seriously.

Let's try and remember that we are people having thoughts. We are not our thoughts.

If we understand this, we can learn to observe our thoughts and choose which ones to engage with.

If we do this, we have more control of our lives. We can start to get our own act together and achieve a certain amount of calmness and joy.

If we can demonstrate that we can live lives of purpose, calmness, and joy, then we can influence those around us in a positive way.

Reflection: What Are Your Thoughts About The World Right Now?

I think we are experiencing a certain amount of uncertainty and chaos right now. You may or may not agree with me on this.

When I focus on this, I start to worry about the future. I worry for my family, my young grandchildren and even the future of the planet.

Perhaps you think like this too sometimes?

What Can Be Done?

If you are like me, you may have lots of ideas about what our government and other people in power should be doing.

You might feel one political party stands more of a chance of changing things for the better than another political party.

Perhaps you don't believe governments can help, or even wish to change things in the way you think things should be changed.

If you are thinking along these lines, then the world can seem a scary, frustrating place to be at times.

How can we bring about positive change then?

That is what this book is about.

If we want to change things, we need to realise how powerful we are.

Change comes from within us, from our ideas and actions.

Chapter 4: What Can We Do To Change Things For The Better?

If we accept that we can observe our thoughts and act upon the useful ones, we can make positive changes in our own lives.

If people around us notice this, they will start to be influenced by us. They will begin to become more aware of their thoughts and choose which thoughts they wish to act upon.

In turn, those people can have a positive impact on people close to them.

Those people can influence people that they interact with and so on.

I like to think of it a bit like when you throw a pebble into a pond.

When you throw the pebble into the pond, ripples start to emerge and move out across the surface of the water.

Actions:

Realising that we can choose to keep hold of some thoughts and let others go, is one thing. Remembering and acting upon this realisation is another.

I have been studying personal development for years now.

Everything that makes sense to me I try and make use of. I tend to write down good strategies and try and use them in my own life.

Some strategies work well for me, while others don't. I keep using the ones that work and put aside the others.

I like to think of it as if I am rooting through a massive toolbox full of tools. Each tool is made for a different purpose. I pick out the tool that I think is best for the job I have ahead of me. If that tool doesn't work, I pack it away and try another. You can do the same.

I have discovered strategies and remedies that work for me. Other people have searched through the same toolbox and found other remedies and strategies that work for them.

We are all unique individuals, so what works well for one person, may not work so well for another.

Chapter 5: Knowing When To Ask For Help

At this point, I must point out that the strategies and ideas suggested in this book are no substitute for you consulting health professionals and other experts when you need support.

If you are in any doubt about trying a strategy or approach, then ask your doctor for their opinion. They are qualified to give you the advice that you need.

Chapter 6: Our Spheres Of Influence

We all have our own spheres of influence.

First of all, we have responsibility for ourselves. We need to make sure that we are OK, and then we are in a better position to help those close to us.

Imagine a drawing of you as a stick person standing in a circle. There is another larger circle drawn around that circle and another larger circle drawn around that. You are in circle 1.

Circle 2 has you in your circle, together with your loved ones.

Loved ones can comprise of family members, friends, colleagues, and people that we meet in our lives. These are people that we tend to spend time with and can have a big impact on.

Circle 3 has both those smaller circles and other people that we have some influence on.

Each of us has other people that matter to us, but we connect with them less than we do with the people in Circle 2.

Again, it's a bit like that pebble causing rippling of water in the pond, in this case you are the pebble. You are going to have the biggest impact on those closest to you, but your influence can reach out further across that pond.

Hopefully, this shows that our actions and words do have an impact on many other people.

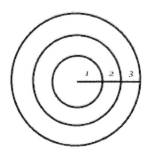

Chapter 7: We Can Make A Difference

It can help us to remember when we are feeling down that we really do make a difference in the world.

With all the crazy goings on that we see on The News, it can appear that there's nothing we can do about all kinds of potential challenges and disasters that may or may not be in the pipeline.

I know I have been affected by this. I have had to make a conscious effort to remind myself that there are things that I can have an impact on and things that I can't change.

Something that I had neglected until recently, is to remember how our thoughts affect our feelings and actions. Our actions influence people around us. We don't have to argue with people and try and prove that we are right. If we live our lives in a way that we feel comfortable with, our actions are likely to positively impact the people around us.

Listening to other people and finding ways to communicate effectively are important aspects of this. If we listen to people and we try to understand them, they are more likely to listen to us and be positively influenced by us.

If they are also able to live a life that they feel happy with, they are more likely to positively influence other people that they know, and so on.

Creativity:

One way that we can influence people is by creating things. Some people make art, other people act, other people create music. Some people are fantastic at gardening and create wonderful gardens. Other people are good at baking and create delicious food. We all have our unique skills and talents that we can bring and share in the world.

Community:

Community is also very important.

It is great to have people around you who understand you and respect you and in turn, you understand and respect them.

Communication:

The way that we communicate with one another is so important.

When we truly listen to other people and try and see things from their perspective, we connect better with them, and we begin to understand them better.

Dreams:

It's vital to have dreams.

Never forget to dream.

Sometimes life can be stressful. It is so important to balance this out with having exciting dreams.

I have a dream that I am going to share with you now.

My Dream:

The thought that prompted me to get writing today was, 'What if I wrote a book about my hopes and dreams?'

What if people bought my book and found out about my dream and liked the idea?

Sharing my ideas is likely to improve the chances of me turning my dreams into reality.

What if people reading this book helped them to follow their dreams?

Writing this down helps me feel clearer about my hopes and dreams.

Hopefully, people reading the book would realise that they can work on their dreams too.

If we all take steps towards positive change, it would show that if we work together, we can achieve just about anything.

Chapter 8: Dreaming

Let me tell you more about my dream.

My dream is to open a wellbeing centre by the sea in the United Kingdom. I would like it to provide a vegetarian café where the food is both healthy and good value. There would be space for artists to come and create, as well as space for musicians to gather and perform.

There would also be room for group and individual life coaching sessions.

There would be a small animal sanctuary as well as glamping accommodation for visitors.

I would live close by in a cosy cabin and would put my energy and efforts into supporting each element of the centre, as well as writing about personal development in order to pass on what I learn to others.

The people running the facilities would be valued for their unique skills and talents. The visitors would receive support and inspiration, and the local community would benefit from a thriving organisation that supports local businesses.

The profits from the book could be used to support elements of this dream.

I also wish to support a wonderful animal sanctuary that I know of. It would be great to be able to support them with their running costs.

Do you remember I mentioned that I wanted to support a worthy cause?

'Wanderers Haven' is the sanctuary that I am talking about.

I will tell you more about them soon.

Chapter 9: Do Things Differently

I woke up in the middle of the night because of a thought that was forming in my head.

I acknowledged that I have a seemingly impossible dream but is it really impossible?

With sufficient funding I could open the centre. I could focus on one area at a time.

I think that this might be possible, and so I have decided to try.

As Henry Ford said, 'If you always do what you've always done, you'll always get what you've always got.'

If I want a different result I need to do things differently. I need to put all the things that I have been learning into practise to see if I can make my seemingly impossible dream a reality.

Each chapter of this book will explain a little more of what could be achieved.

This book isn't just about my dream. It is about yours too. As you read about my dream, think about your own too. Consider what steps you could take to make your dream a reality.

The Start:

I will start by publishing this book and letting my friends know about it.

If 100 of them each decide to buy a copy of the book and let another two people know about it, the information written here would spread quickly.

Look how numbers increase rapidly when two people tell two more people about something and those two people tell two more….

1 person tells…

2 people and they tell 2 more…

This increases to:

4

8

16

32

64

128

256

512

1024

2048

4096

8192

16384

262144

524288

1048576…

So, starting with 2 people telling 2 more people, look at how fast the number of people increases. In a few steps you have more than a million people!

Isn't it amazing?

This concept is exciting.

Think about how quickly some video's 'go viral' on social media.

If you have a good idea and spread the word in this way, you can make a real impact in the world.

I have lots of ideas about ways a wellbeing centre could run. I realise that each of the elements needs thought and consideration.

I also believe that ideas need to be flexible if dreams are to become reality.

Let's look more closely at the main elements of my dream.

Chapter 10: The Wellbeing Centre

What could it offer?

Firstly, I would love there to be a café.

 Let's start with the café.

The café seems central to the project.

 I believe that every community benefits from a café serving delicious, nutritious, and affordable food. I would love to offer a vegetarian café using locally sourced ingredients, where possible.

Running the café, cooking, and serving the food would be a rewarding job for the right people who are passionate about good food and the importance of Community.

The café would need to be affordable and could even offer recipe cards and cooking events to encourage people to cook more for themselves. Some food would be gluten free, and we would cater for other special diets.

A café is a great place for people to meet, chat and support one another.

Unfortunately, since Lockdown a lot of cafés have struggled to keep going and have closed down. I would love to reopen a lovely little café somewhere. It is sad when old buildings get run down and communities start to decline.

We have to think it is possible for things to improve. If we think it is possible, we can improve things together.

Chapter 11: Boosting Happiness

I think our happiness levels could also do with a boost.

There are all sorts of ways we can increase our happiness.

Have you heard of 'Action For Happiness?'

If you haven't, visit their website to find out more about them:

https://actionforhappiness.org/

They are trying to make the world a happier, kinder place.

I love this concept.

They have a pledge: 'I will try to create more happiness and less unhappiness around me.'

That is what I try to do. I see other people doing this in all kinds of lovely ways.

Action For Happiness encourage the creation of 'Happy Café's where people know they can go to receive support and companionship. I definitely think a wellbeing centre could adopt this idea.

We will be exploring what else 'Action For Happiness' demonstrates a little later.

Now, let's move on to how music and art can enhance what could be offered at the centre.

Music:

What is your favourite song?

Just about everyone enjoys music. Music can unite and inspire people.

I greatly admire local musicians who put on free events in pubs and cafés. I would love to offer a venue for musicians to come and perform. After Lockdown, a lot of music venues closed. This is very sad. Music is so uplifting and a vital part of life.

Gigs and other evenings of music could be hosted in a wellbeing centre. This would be entertaining for audience and performers alike. It would also be great to have rooms available for people to have music lessons, singing lessons and to practise for performances.

Art:

Art is wonderful to create and admire. Local artists could teach people to paint at the centre. They could also display and potentially sell their work at exhibitions that the centre could host. It would be great to allow children to attend art and music workshops, and we could also put on events that cater for older people.

Coaching:

One thing I love to do is coach. The centre could offer a room suitable for hosting coaching events for small groups and individuals. That is something I would be excited to get involved in. We could potentially offer writing workshops too. The possibilities are endless!

The most important thing would be to make events affordable and accessible to all.

Animal Sanctuary:

Another important element of the project is the animal sanctuary. Animals offer us so much and many require rehoming through no fault of their own. I would love to offer a sanctuary where we could house some animals and look for loving homes for others. This could be run as a charity or not-for-profit organisation.

People would hopefully be willing to fundraise to support the animals including covering essential costs such as vet bills etc.

Young people are likely to benefit from work experience at the sanctuary and older people would also have much to contribute here.

Gardening:

It would be great to be able to grow some of our own food including growing fruit trees. People visiting the centre could learn how to grow their own fruit and vegetables.

Education:

The whole centre would be educational. We could recycle and reuse things and encourage others to do likewise. We could have solar panels and small wind turbines available to help us to generate some clean energy.

People could donate old books that they have finished reading and so we could offer a mini library.

Wellbeing:

How would such a centre be good for our wellbeing?

Let's return to 'Action For Happiness' here:

If you visit their website, you will learn about, The 10 Keys.

Together they spell GREAT DREAM.

Let's explore each aspect of this:

G- Giving.

Do kind things for others. When we do kind things for others, we feel better ourselves.

R-Relating.

Relating to others. It is important for us to connect with people.

E- Exercising.

Take care of your body.

A-Awareness.

Live life mindfully.

T-Trying out.

Keep learning new things.

D-Direction.

Have goals to look forward to.

R-Resilience.

Find ways to bounce back.

E-Emotions.

Look for what's good.

A-Acceptance.

Be comfortable with who you are.

M-Meaning.

Be part of something bigger.

Think of all the good thoughts here. This organisation is dedicated to helping people take steps to feel happier.

Let's consider how these keys could apply to a wellbeing centre:

How would a wellbeing centre help people to be happier in their lives?

Let's explore the philosophy.

I have found that focusing on each of the 10 Keys greatly enhances my own life and the lives of others.

Let's consider how the centre would help us follow these principles.

Giving: There would be plenty of opportunities for giving. People could meet and buy delicious food for people that they care about. They could create art pieces to give away to people too.

 Relating: There would be great opportunities for people to connect through food, art, music, their love of animals and by having the opportunity to camp together.

People could share time out in nature and likeminded people could create and share music together.

 Exercising: There would be lovely exercise opportunities including walking the sanctuary animals, gardening, and walking in nature.

Awareness: Awareness is another important key. Mindful eating could be demonstrated, and mindfulness could be brought into the coaching experience.

Trying Out: Trying out is another wonderful key. Visitors could be invited to try cooking, art, music, gardening, and writer's workshops enhanced by an enjoyable glamping experience.

Direction: Direction would be important too. People could set personal goals in the coaching workshops and be involved in setting goals for the centre to achieve as well.

Resilience: Resilience is another important key. Running a thriving community takes commitment and the ability to bounce back from setbacks.

Emotions: Noticing what is good in the world can give our mood a lift. Being around people willing to listen to and understand us is so important and this is something the centre could offer.

Accepting: Accepting all our emotions is another important key.

Coaching sessions encourage honesty, openness, and good listening skills.

Acceptance is an important key, and this can be fostered at the centre. Having somewhere for support groups to meet would encourage and support people in reaching a state of acceptance.

Meaning: Meaning is the final key. I believe that the facilities offered by such a centre would provide a meaningful experience to our visitors.

As with all families, mine has had its share of happiness and sadness. A recent, unexpected bereavement prompted me to do something to lift my spirits. I discovered the 'Action For Happiness' talks and found them to be inspiring and uplifting.

Some of the speakers have written personal development books that I have got a lot out of, and I decided that I wanted to give something back.

I have become an Action For Happiness volunteer and help run their online courses.

Our centre would be a great place to offer to run 'Action For Happiness' groups and other events.

Chapter 12: Challenges

We're living in challenging times. Views are often polarised, particularly on social media.

The rich appear to get richer while the poor seem to get poorer. People feel isolated and don't always find the time to listen to and learn from one another.

Each person is unique and has their own gifts to offer the world. I think we can sometimes tend to forget this. We see celebrities on TV and start to believe their views are more important than ours. We can think that we don't have much to offer. This couldn't be further from the truth.

A wellbeing centre provides an opportunity for people to share their skills and learn from one another, it would be fantastic to provide meaningful employment for a number of local people.

It might be possible to form a worker's cooperative so that staff have a say in the way things are run.

The centre could be created from an old disused pub, hotel, bed and breakfast, or café.

Many such businesses have struggled over the past few years, and it would be wonderful to put a fabulous old building to good use again.

The centre would provide a cosy place for people to meet and support one another.

Chapter 13: Generations

Generations can benefit from spending time together and learning from one another.

Young children gain so much from the wisdom of grandparents while grandparents become uplifted and feel valued in the presence of younger people.

The centre would also provide an opportunity for older people to get together and share their life experiences. They could attend a regular get-together session.

Young people could attend a youth club and both groups could enjoy joining in shared activities perhaps fund-raising events to provide for the animals in the sanctuary, for example.

Unity:

Imagine one million people collaborating to create somewhere positive and uniting for people to visit.

Maybe some would visit the centre once it opened, knowing that they helped make a difference to the many visitors that will benefit from visiting.

Perhaps they could decide to participate in the virtual wellbeing café that is already in existence.

I created 'Cathy's Virtual Wellbeing Café' on Facebook three years ago tomorrow. (15th May 2021)

It's a supportive place for people to visit and communicate with each other.

I decided that I loved the concept of a wellbeing café and while I hadn't got the funds to create a physical one, I realised that there were many benefits to offering a virtual one.

People love getting together, talking about the things that they enjoy and discovering the hopes and dreams of their fellow visitors.

When turning a dream into a reality it is good to have a prototype, I feel.

I can see how beneficial the virtual café is and it convinces me of the benefits of having a physical one.

Here is a link to 'Cathy's Virtual Wellbeing Café.'

You are very welcome to join us here:

Think about your dream. Consider each aspect of your dream in turn and see if you can imagine what things would be like.

In celebration of Cathy's Virtual Wellbeing Café's Third birthday, I have decided to publish this book!

Chapter 14: Inspiration

We can be inspired by what people are doing now. If they can do it, we can do it.

I have seen aspects of the wellbeing centre operating in the world right at this moment. This is how I know it can be done.

I am inspired by the following:

Café:

There is a wonderful café called Café Atma, in Hythe.

The food is vegetarian, affordable and delicious. The scenery is beautiful, and the staff are friendly.

https://www.facebook.com/brockhillcafe/?locale=en_GB

Visiting a lovely place like this inspires me and shows me that a venture like this is possible.

 Music:

Hippie Joe from Hay Seed Dixie has shown how music can unite generations.

 He plays in his band but also offers 'Live And Unsigned' evenings to provide a platform for local talent.

If you want to find out more, you can visit the website:

https://hayseed-dixie.com/the-band/

 I have attended many uplifting events organised by him in local venues in Essex.

This is the kind of thing that could also be offered at a wellbeing centre.

Art:

Sienna Rose Projects or Kerry's Art Studio demonstrates how enjoyable creating art can be. Kerry's Facebook page shows some of the lovely projects she offers in her local area of Kent.

 I have joined garland making workshops in a cosy pub, and poppy painting in a lovely café, for example. The venue benefits from customers and the customer benefits from the pleasure of getting together and creating art. This kind of thing could definitely be offered at a wellbeing centre.

https://www.facebook.com/siennaroseproducts

 Wanderers Haven Animal Sanctuary inspires me too.

The staff and volunteers work tirelessly to provide secure happy homes for the abandoned animals.

For every £1 profit made in sales from this book, 50p will be donated to Wanderers Haven.

Visit their Facebook page to find out more about the wonderful work they do:

https://www.facebook.com/wanderershavenanimalsanctuary/?locale=en_GB

It would be wonderful to offer something similar at a wellbeing centre. It would start small, ensuring that the animals that are taken in are well looked after.

Visitors to the centre would help to support the animals and in turn they would benefit from knowing that they have made a difference to the lives of the animals changing things for the better.

Experience:

I have set up a charity in the past and so I have some knowledge of how to set one up.

In 1994 I ran a family drop-in centre in Hastings called Kids Galore.

This was a place where families could go for companionship, cost price food and support.

I really enjoyed running this charity and I'm very grateful to the people that helped me. We had a chairperson, treasurer, and secretary as well as a management committee. An accountant kept our books for us as we raised money to go on outings and buy equipment for the children to play on.

We also offered interesting workshops that benefited the families. Learning how to set up a charity was invaluable to me, so I know that if was decided to set up a not-for-profit or charity to run a sanctuary, this is something that is achievable.

Online:

During the pandemic, cafés and other meeting places had to close. Everything moved online. I attended lots of online events including a couch choir where I sang along while sat on my sofa. Many people started working from home. We all did the best that we could.

There is still a place for online events, zoom and other video calls to help us stay in touch, but there is no substitute for face-to-face contact.

People become lonely and isolated if they do not have the opportunity to meet other people. A high number of cafés and other venues have shut down. This is sad.

I would love to help breathe new life into a venue. I believe it would become a much-needed hub for people to meet, discuss and share ideas.

I would love to offer opportunities for groups to meet and support their members. It's so important for people who have things in common to get the chance to get together.

It's equally important to allow different people to mix. If you take time to listen to other people you understand them better. We don't all have to agree. We can learn to agree to disagree. This is so important now.

It would be wonderful to offer comfortable cabins for people to stay in. That way, we could offer events such as themed weekends.

I love coaching people using audio and video calls. There's also a need for a suitable room to offer face to face low-cost coaching for groups and individuals. The key is affordability. There are some amazing spas and retreats available, but the costs can be prohibitive to many.

Dreaming out Loud:

People who know me will probably have heard of my dream of opening a wellbeing centre by the sea. I have been talking about this dream with people that I know for quite a while now.

Cathy's Virtual Wellbeing Café is my virtual prototype.

I will be having a launch party there tomorrow where I will let people know about this book.

I am inspired and uplifted by art, music, coaching, camping and animals. They could combine in a Wellbeing Centre.

I have decided to try and develop each aspect of the idea further.

I don't know if I will achieve this dream, but I am willing to try.

If you join my virtual wellbeing cafe on Facebook, I will be able to post any progress updates there.

If you have a dream, it is important to be open to the possibility of it coming true.

If people know about your dream and they like the idea then they might be able to help you.

Chapter 15: Possible?

This chapter is a bit different. It is dreaming into the future. It is describing a possible scenario for the future:
Imagine this as a diary entry and consider if this could actually happen.
I have written entries in a diary as if my dream has come true. You could do the same.
 Doing this can help you to imagine things more vividly and you can become much clearer on your goals.
In reality, things might turn out differently but that is fine. It is great to be open to ideas and opportunities and not be too fixated on specific details.
Things can turn out even better than you imagine!

Diary Entry:

It was amazing how things turned out following the 'Notice The Good Things' experiment in May 2024.

I started by rating how I was feeling about key aspects of my life and I invited followers and friends on my social media pages to do likewise.

I thought about each area of my life:

Work

Home

Interests

Spirituality

Physical aspects of life

Emotional aspects of life

Relationships

Security

I came up with a rough score out of 10. My score was 6.

I decided that every day for the first 2 weeks of May I would actively look out for 6 good things.

After that I decided to rate my life again and see if actively noticing what is good in the world boosted my score at all.

I discovered by looking out for good things happening even on fairly stressful days I noticed more and more good things in my life.

I was delighted that other people joined in with this challenge and rated their own lives out of 10.

Whatever the number they came up with was the number of good things they looked out for each day. People who had a low score had less good things to look out for. This was less intimidating for them, and they found that they started to find more and more good things about their lives as the challenge proceeded.

I was so excited at the positive impact this challenge had on people that I included some key findings in my book.

In early June I published my book. I felt excited and hopeful.

I was determined to promote the book through word of mouth as much as much as possible.

I figured that if I could get 100 of my friends to 'Buy one, tell two and review ' we could spread the word.

It is incredible how quickly book sales started to grow!

I didn't want to make the book too expensive. I decided that I was happy with £1 profit per book. Fifty pence would go to the animal sanctuary and 50p would be put towards developing the wellbeing centre idea.

I planned some mini breaks with my partner and dogs at various places on the coast in order to see where we could potentially open the centre. I figured that if I believed this project might succeed, I needed to have some idea about a possible location for the centre.

I was determined not to be too fixed location or venue so that I would be open to unexpected places becoming available.

This was a fun and relaxing thing to do, and it helped us explore and get to know coastal areas better. We found some areas were picturesque but expensive and other areas more affordable.

It was exciting and a little scary when the book sales grew so quickly. I opened a separate bank account for the centre.

I updated the members of my virtual café. We formed a group of like-minded people who all expressed an interest in helping to get the project off the ground.

People made suggestions on places to visit that might be worth investigating.

One exciting suggestion involved a pub close to the beach that had gone out of business and was being sold.

At this point I actually started to truly believe that the project had a chance.

My partner and I booked into a holiday chalet one weekend and we arranged to view the pub.

As we approached, my heart started pounding with excitement. It almost felt as if I had been there before.

The pub hadn't been shut for long.

When we were shown inside, we could see that it had been well maintained. The bar area had enough room for musical performances.

The estate agent told us that the previous owners had held music nights and there were no neighbours close enough to be bothered by the noise.

I noticed there was a good-sized carpark, a field, and a number of outbuildings that would be suitable for workshops and for our animal sanctuary.

The look on my partners face told me all that I needed to know. He had been supportive and encouraging of my crazy plan but had doubted that a suitable place could be found and as we walked round the property the emerging smile on his face told me that he thought we had found the place for us. After we had viewed the whole place, the agent left us, and we went for a little walk along the cliff path into a nearby wood. The whole place seemed oddly familiar, and I felt like I had arrived home.

The dwelling closest to the pub was a short walk along the path. It was a little holiday cabin. There were three cabins in a row. They each looked charming and cosy. There was a 'To Let' sign in the window of one of them. I took a note of the number as I considered that it would be great to be able to stay close to the pub if we were lucky enough to be able to buy it.

I am delighted to be able to tell you that while I didn't have quite enough money from book sales to offer the asking price, I did make a lower offer and the offer was accepted!

I phoned the number I had noticed in the cabin, and they sent me a booking form. I booked the cabin for a week so my partner and I could travel there and stay in the cabin while sorting out the pub purchase.

The cabin was every bit as cosy and sweet inside as I had imagined it would be.

A group of people from my virtual café agreed to help me with setting up the centre.

A lovely woman called Lisa and her partner were local and were looking for work. They had bar and restaurant experience.

I asked them to meet me at the pub.

I knew as soon as I met them that they would be perfect managers for the centre.

My friend James had experience of running a campsite and agreed to help me set up the glamping side of the wellbeing centre.

It was quite incredible how key aspects of the project started falling into place.

I set up the animal sanctuary as a not-for-profit organisation and a wonderful woman called Sam agreed to spend the summer helping me to set up the animal shelter.

Before long, the sale of the pub was complete, and we were able to open our doors serving drinks and delicious vegetarian food.

Local businesses were very supportive, and we were able to offer a range of local products.

One of the most exciting events was when the owner of the cabin contacted me explaining that they were hoping to sell it. They had heard about me wanting to set up a wellbeing centre and they were in favour of this idea.

For that reason, they offered me the cabin at a reduced rate. I did not hesitate; I accepted their offer and bought the cabin for myself and my partner to stay in.

There were challenges along the way, of course there were, but overall things came together remarkably quickly.

I found a wonderful local artist who was delighted to be able to run painting workshops at the café.

Musicians were happy to rent the small studios we created from some outbuildings. They started rehearsing for a concert they were putting on for our launch.

Local animal charities liaised with us to help us purchase suitable equipment for our sanctuary.

The day the tents and shepherd's huts arrived was one of the most exciting of my life!

I had dreamed of setting up a wellbeing centre for such a long time, but I had imagined that the only way I could raise the necessary funds would be if I won the money. What were the odds of that happening?

Not very high.

Deciding to publish my book about the power of thoughts and giving details about my possible, impossible dream helped to make it all happen!

The concert was wonderful. The musicians were on top form and the local community were very enthusiastic about our achievements.

Not long afterwards, our sanctuary was ready to welcome the first residents.
The very first animal was a wire-haired terrier called Benny.
He was so cute.
His owner was an elderly man who lived alone.
After he died, his daughter contacted us to see if we could offer Benny a home. She couldn't, as her daughter was severely allergic to dog fur.
She had heard about our centre from one of the musicians who was renting a studio at our place.
I am so glad that I decided to give this dream a chance!'

Can you imagine what the centre might be like from reading this description?

If I can imagine something, I feel it is easier for me to believe in it.

If you have a dream, try visualising it. When you can picture something, it is easier to believe that it could happen.

Chapter 16: My Thought Diary
These are actual notes that I took when I came up with the idea for the 'Notice The Good Things Challenge.'
The challenge was planned for May 2024.

Notes:
March 29th:
In May I am taking part in an exciting experiment.
I am going to rate how I feel about my life and the world out of 10.
April:

W Work
H Home
I Interests
S Spirituality
P Physical
E Emotional
R Relationships
S Security
Taking all these aspects of my life into account, I decided that my score was 6/10.

My score is:6.
In May I will consciously look out for the 6 good things each day.
I will record them in my diary and share them on my social media pages in the hope that others will join me.
I will run this challenge for 2 weeks and include the findings in my book. I will rate how I feel about life then and continue with the challenge until the end of May.
On the last day of May, I will rate how I feel about the key aspects of my life once again to see if things have improved. This is testing the suggestion that what you focus on grows.

If we look out for the good things does the world get better?

The News is generally negative, focusing on what is wrong with the world. When we watch it, we can't help worrying about the future.
On social media platforms the algorithm tends to guide us in the direction of people we agree with. The way this works is that when we 'Like' a post expressing a particular opinion it shows us more posts of a similar nature.

If you 'Like ' a post about animals, for example, you are likely to be shown more and more posts about animals.
Advertisers selling products to animal lovers are then able to target a group of animal lovers in one place and so their advertising campaigns are more likely to be successful.

If you spend a lot of time looking at posts from animal lovers, it is easy to believe that most people are animal lovers but someone who dislikes animals is unlikely to 'Like' the same posts as you.
They are more likely to 'Like ' posts that are critical of animals and so the algorithm guides them in a different direction.
The same thing happens with opinions about other things. People who agree with left wing politics see material considered to be left wing while those with right wing views are shown material that is right wing.

Comments in videos shown are likely to match your own. This can lead people to believe that most people feel the way that they do and that people with a different opinion are wrong. This means that if you want to be as balanced as possible, you need to go out of your way to examine alternative opinions.
Once you realise that much of the material you come across is negative and that there are alternative views and experiences to your own, you can become more balanced.
It is important to be able to see things from another person's perspective.

Notice The Good Things Challenge:

In this experiment we are going out of our way to notice good things in the news and in our own lives.
Look out for helpful people who hold doors open for you or go out of their way to help people. Notice the smiley helpful people who do kind things.

On a stressful day, look up and notice that the sun is shining. On a day when something doesn't work out well in one area, look out for something that makes you feel better. It might be a catchy tune that plays on the radio or a delicious cup of coffee that your friend makes you when they came round for a chat.

We are not denying or suppressing the stressful or challenging things, we are actively looking for the rainbow after the rainstorm and the silver lining in every cloud.
When you notice something, write it down so that you remember it.
Look back on your target score. In this example it is 6. Try and record at least that number of good things each day.

Chapter 17: Findings

This is what I discovered from taking part in the 'Notice The Good Things Challenge:

Day 1.

It is wonderful that I get to spend my day off with my friendly cat George. It is sunny today. My coffee was delicious, and I found some fascinating YouTube videos to watch. Spending time writing was uplifting too. (That is 6 good things.)

Today I felt rather flat. I found 6 things that were good, but I awarded the day 4/10 which is lower than my original score of 6.
Saying that and being honest with myself helped. I spent time with my cat on my lap feeling blissful.
I also realised that I had unexpectedly saved around £35 on DIY. That made me smile.
I listened to some binaural beats music, and they did lift my mood.

Day 2.
Today I heard a cuckoo, enjoyed the sunshine and I noticed a courteous driver letting me out of a junction.
I saw lots of beautiful oxeye daisies, heard great music, came away feeling appreciated at work and on the way home I had a beautiful view of the cliffs. My mood is 6/10 up from 4/10 yesterday.

Day 3.

Today I noticed a break in the rain, a smooth journey, a weekend on the horizon, a delicious crumpet, laughter at work and pupils making progress. 6/10

Day 4. Today was a hard day, my knees were rather stiff, but I noticed how refreshing my cup of tea was.
I love knowing I have a holiday on Monday.
I enjoyed the sunshine, the rain didn't spoil our walk and watching a programme about Orangutans was interesting. I am enjoying spending time with the dogs. Today is 5/10.

Day 5.

I noticed how lucky I am having free time, being with the dogs, laughing with my partner, having someone who loves cooking doing the cooking and I also noticed that I was enjoying unexpected sunshine and thoroughly enjoyed reading some interesting books. 6/10

Day 6.

I have noticed how cosy I am with my blanket, my cat, and my heater. I have noticed the rhythmic sound of the rain on the roof and am happy knowing I don't have to go anywhere on this cold, rainy day. I appreciate my mug of coffee. My happiness score is currently 7/10.

Day 7.

I have noticed how relaxing binaural beats are.
It stopped raining when I went outside.
 My blanket keeps me warm so I can let the cat have the door open which makes him happy. Thinking about the programme The Piano makes me smile. Manuka honey in my earl grey tea is delicious. I award today 7/10.

I have been much more aware of my thoughts and feelings this week and realise how many thoughts pass through my mind. I seem to focus on a thought, it gets more powerful and takes up energy. If I realise it isn't a thought that I wish to dwell on, I tell myself it is just a thought. I focus on my breath and the thought gets replaced by another.

Day 8.
 My vegetable crisps are delicious. There are many caring people on X trying to help improve life for others, music is so uplifting, so is birdsong.
 My cat purring is so relaxing, and my exercise bike lets me exercise whenever I feel like it. I award today 8/10.

Day 9.
I noticed lovely birds in my garden, field campions in the verges and incredibly, what I thought was a crack on the car windscreen wiped off!
The Action For Happiness video I watched was very good. It is about Mindfulness, The guy at the petrol station was friendly and I have enjoyed a delicious hot chocolate. I was remarkably calm over the suspected windscreen chip. I think noticing the good things is having a noticeable positive impact even during stressful episodes. I awarded today 8/10 again.
Day 10.
Considering I have serious car troubles I am pleased I noticed 6 good things today! My clutch failed. I was safe despite the road being busy. When I managed to get home my neighbour helped me. The radio kept me calm and entertained while I was dealing with the car issues. I am fortunate this happened at the weekend, My cat was happy to see me when I got home and my friend has offered to help if I need her. I award today 6/10.

Day 11.
 Today saw me noticing the kindness of my friends and my neighbours. My partner is my support and sounding board. Pictures of the Northern Lights seen in UK last night are beautiful. The salesperson at the garage was friendly and helpful. My new car is driving well, and I am getting a good price for the previous one. I award today 9/10. It held its share

of stressors but noticing the good while accepting the challenges is really helping me.

Stop press. Once you start looking out for the good things you find more and more. Today the recovery truck driver moving my car got blocked in by an ice-cream van but instead of getting stressed he laughed it off and offered to buy me an ice-cream!

Day 12.

The more I notice good things, the better things seem to appear. I found an author who has written a new book about Happiness, it sounds great. Music is uplifting today, along with the sunshine. My clothes are drying quickly, lots of people are joining my Notice The Good Things Challenge and I have a good idea for a video celebration for Cathy's Wellbeing Café's 3rd Birthday on 15th May.

 I award today 9/10. I am feeling uplifted.

Day 13.

My friend at work was attentive when I told her about my car adventures,

Today I loved driving my new car, I saw a lovely horse on my route home and I noticed some beautiful poppies. My partner's van passed its MOT. A work meeting went well and the pasty I ate for my dinner was delicious. I award today 9/10. I found it hard to choose which good things to note down as there were so many.

Day 14.

Spending time with George Cat is a great thing. Painting with friends is wonderful. I am so happy Cathy's Wellbeing Café celebrates its 3rd birthday tomorrow. I am delighted my book draft is ready. I am ready to publish. Today I painted a cabin that I have decided to use as the front cover illustration for my book. Listening to the rain on my caravan roof is remarkably relaxing and binaural beats are inspiring. Today has to be a 10/10!

I will continue with this challenge until the end of May and will rate how I feel about life then.

At this precise moment I rate life at 9/10.

This is a remarkable shift from 6/10.

This happened despite some challenges and stresses and helps me realise that noticing the good things can really offer comfort and support during challenging times.

Chapter 18:

Now I am ready to publish this book. I will post updates on social media so that you know how the experiment is working out.

I will also post on Substack. If you subscribe to my Substack newsletter it will be emailed to you so you can follow the progress:

https://cathyshuter.substack.com/

Thanks for reading this. I hope it inspires you to follow some dreams of your own!

Please remember that your thoughts are very powerful. You can choose the thoughts that you wish to focus on, and you can find ways to accept and then release the thoughts that aren't helping you.

This will help you feel happier and more in control of your life.

Good luck and enjoy the adventure!

Printed in Great Britain
by Amazon

41937043R00030